My First Animal Library

Prairie Dogs

by Cari Meister

Bullfrog Books

Ideas for Parents and Teachers

Bullfrog Books let children practice reading informational text at the earliest reading levels. Repetition, familiar words, and photo labels support early readers.

Before Reading

- Discuss the cover photo. What does it tell them?
- Look at the picture glossary together. Read and discuss the words.

Read the Book

- "Walk" through the book and look at the photos. Let the child ask questions. Point out the photo labels.
- Read the book to the child, or have him or her read independently.

After Reading

- Prompt the child to think more. Ask: Prairie dog towns can be found in central and western grasslands in the United States. Have you ever visited one? What did you see?

Bullfrog Books are published by Jump!
5357 Penn Avenue South
Minneapolis, MN 55419
www.jumplibrary.com

Library of Congress Cataloging-in-Publication Data

Names: Meister, Cari, author.
Title: Prairie dogs / by Cari Meister.
Other titles: Bullfrog books. My first animal library.
Description: Minneapolis, MN : Jump!, Inc., [2018]
Series: My first animal library | Audience: Ages 5–8. Audience: K to grade 3. | Includes index.
Identifiers: LCCN 2017042580 | 9781624967634 (ebook)
ISBN 9781624967627 (hardcover : alk. paper)
Subjects: LCSH: Prairie dogs—Juvenile literature.
Classification: LCC QL737.R68 M455 2019
DDC 599.36/7—dc23
LC record available at https://lccn.loc.gov/2017042580

Editor: Jenna Trnka
Book Designer: Leah Sanders

Photo Credits: Eric Isselee/Shutterstock, cover, 1; Colette3/Shutterstock, 3; Nick Biemans/Shutterstock, 4; Craig Hosterman/Shutterstock, 5; tomolson54/iStock, 6–7; Nick Saunders/Getty, 8–9, 23mr; bartvdd/iStock, 10–11; Marie Dirgova/Shutterstock, 12, 23br; Robert Olenick/Getty, 13, 23bl; Ron Rowan Photography/Shutterstock, 14–15; DEA PICTURE LIBRARY/Getty, 16 (sign), 23ml; Vilkas Vision/Shutterstock, 16–17 (background); TungCheung/Shutterstock, 16–17 (post); Rod Beverley/Shutterstock, 18; Greg and Jan Ritchie/Shutterstock, 19; Henk Bentlage/Shutterstock, 20–21; Baitong Sathitkun/Shutterstock, 22, 24; Paul Tessier/Shutterstock, 23tl.

Printed in the United States of America at Corporate Graphics in North Mankato, Minnesota.

Table of Contents

Work and Play

A prairie dog greets his sister.

They nuzzle.

They chatter.

They run.

They jump and play.

A prairie dog is not a dog.

It is a rodent.

But it yips like a dog.

It has sharp teeth.

It eats grass.

It eats seeds
and roots.

Prairie dogs are social.
They share food.

They groom each other.

See the long nails?
They are sharp.
They dig tunnels.

nails

PRAIRIE DOG TOWN
lookout mound
food
sleeping room
nursery

The tunnels have chambers.

They are like rooms.

They connect.

It is a dog town.

This one stands guard.
He listens for danger.

He alerts the group.

They hide!

It is safe now.

They go back to work.

Parts of a Prairie Dog

Picture Glossary

alerts
Warns others of danger or a threat.

chambers
Underground rooms connected by tunnels.

groom
To clean the fur.

nuzzle
To rub gently against the nose and mouth.

rodent
A gnawing mammal with sharp front teeth.

social
Living together in groups with a form of communication between each other.

Index

To Learn More

Learning more is as easy as 1, 2, 3.

1) Go to www.factsurfer.com

2) Enter "prairiedogs" into the search box.

3) Click the "Surf" button to see a list of websites.

With factsurfer.com, finding more information is just a click away.

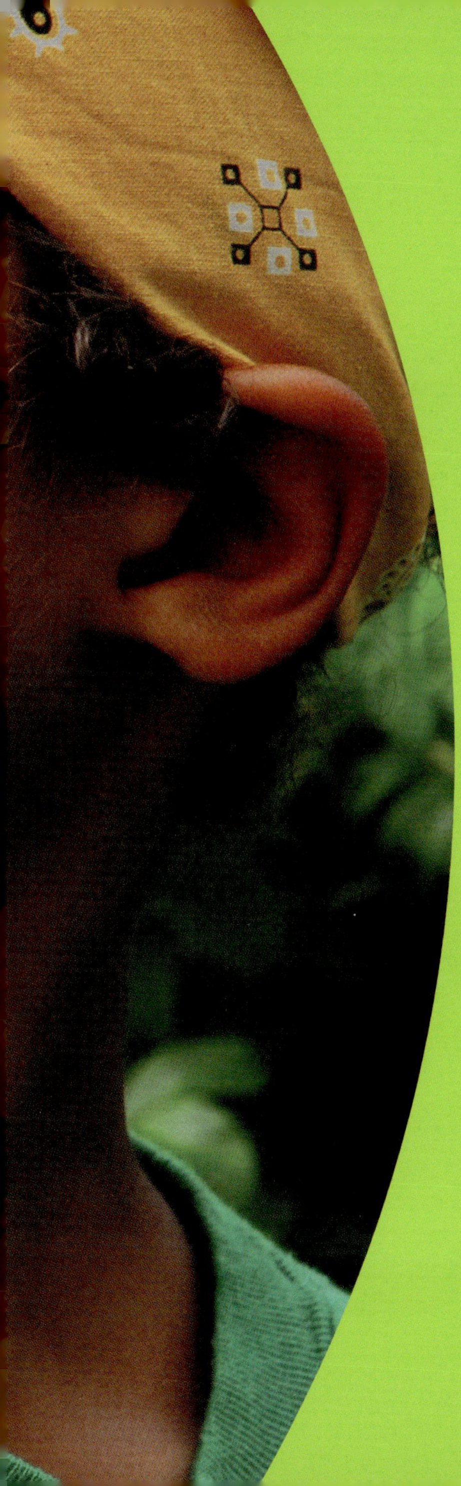

Lizards are cool pets!

What Does a Lizard Need?

tank
Make sure it is big enough for your lizard to move around comfortably.

heat source
Lizards are cold-blooded. They need a heat source to keep them warm.

hiding place
Lizards need a place to hide and feel safe.

rocks
Lizards like to rest on rocks.

water dish
A big shallow dish is best.

food
Different lizards eat different things; check with a vet to see what is best.

Picture Glossary

ackie
A desert lizard that is part of the monitor family.

bask
To lie or relax in a pleasant warmth.

bearded dragon
A medium-sized lizard with a triangular head and spiny scales.

crested
Having protruding ridges.

gecko
A tropical lizard that eats insects and is active at night.

tegu
A large lizard that is native to Central and South America.

Index

To Learn More

Learning more is as easy as 1, 2, 3.

1) Go to www.factsurfer.com

2) Enter "petlizards" into the search box.

3) Click the "Surf" button to see a list of websites.

With factsurfer.com, finding more information is just a click away.